P9-EFI-966

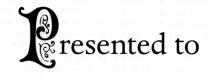

Presented to

_____

BY

_____

ON

_____

the Nativity Story

Tyndale House Publishers, Inc., Carol Stream, Illinois

Visit Tyndale's exciting Web site at www.tyndale.com

TYNDALE and Tyndale's quill logo are registered trademarks of Tyndale House Publishers, Inc.

The Nativity Story

Copyright © MMVI New Line Productions, Inc.

Photographs by Jaimie Trueblood. All photographs © MMVI New Line Productions, Inc.

Art directed by Jacqueline L. Noe

Designed by Jennifer Ghionzoli

Edited by Stephanie Voiland

Scripture quotations are taken from the *Holy Bible*, New Living Translation, copyright © 1996, 2004. Used by permission of Tyndale House Publishers, Inc., Carol Stream, Illinois 60188. All rights reserved.

ISBN-13: 978-1-4143-1463-1

ISBN-10: 1-4143-1463-9

Printed in the United States

12 11 10 09 08 07 06

7 6 5 4 3 2 1

able of Contents

God Is with Us

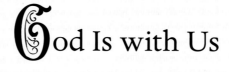

On a starry night, some two thousand years ago, a baby boy took His first breath.

There was nothing dramatic about it, at first glance. The occasion was marked by the quietness of a rural village and attended by a rather common assortment of people. Breaking into the stillness of that evening was a sound that echoed countless births before this one: the sound of a newborn's cry.

Babies make their entrance into the world in less than idyllic fashion. Their arrivals tend to be unscheduled, painful, and messy...

and ordinary to all but a precious few.

In those respects, this baby was no different. In fact, His birth was even less glamorous than most. No midwives, no birthing room, no extended family to celebrate. Just an earthy animal shelter to shield against the night air and a rough feeding trough for Him to sleep in.

And yet there was something in the air... something intangible, something startling and achingly beautiful. Did everyone sense it? Or was it only those with expectant hearts, longing souls?

Years later, traces of that night still linger. And those among us with expectant hearts and longing souls can catch a glimpse, if we are willing to gaze through fresh eyes—the eyes of those whose lives were woven into the story of that wonder-filled night.

See through the eyes of Elizabeth, who recognized something extraordinary about this baby, even before He was born.

See through the eyes of Zechariah, who saw that this child would be the rescuer we were waiting for, the answer to God's promise.

See through the eyes of John, the child's cousin, who one day would prepare the world to meet Him.

See through the eyes of King Herod, whose jealousy of this baby drove him to brutal extremes.

See through the eyes of the shepherds, who never expected to find themselves ushering in history's most dramatic miracle.

See through the eyes of the Magi, whose search for truth led them from a distant country to the feet of their King.

See through the eyes of a hardworking carpenter, who would fill in as the child's father, for the moment.

See through the eyes of a peasant girl, the child's mother, whose fears were stilled in the presence of simple faith and pure love.

And see through the eyes of the Messiah Himself, who put flesh on the promise that, for now and for all eternity, God is with us.

Let us see through new eyes, allowing the miracle of that night—and what it means for us all—to fill our hearts with joy and hope.

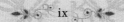

The Lord

himself will give you the sign.

Look!

The virgin will conceive a child!

She will give birth to a son and will call him

Immanuel

(which means "God is with us").

Isaiah 7:14

Mary

VILLAGE OF NAZARETH

"For the time is coming,"
*says the L*ORD,
"when I will raise up a righteous descendant
from King David's line.
He will be a King who rules with wisdom.
He will do what is just and right throughout the land.
And this will be his name:
*'The L*ORD *Is Our Righteousness.'*
In that day Judah will be saved,
and Israel will live in safety."

Jeremiah 23:5-6

Magi

PALACE IN THE PERSIAN EMPIRE

I see him, but not here and now.
I perceive him, but far in the distant future.
A star will rise from Jacob;
a scepter will emerge from Israel. . . .
A ruler will rise in Jacob.

Numbers 24:17, 19

I will make you a light to the Gentiles,
and you will bring my salvation to the ends of the earth. . . .
Kings will stand at attention when you pass by.
Princes will also bow low
because of the LORD, the faithful one,
the Holy One of Israel, who has chosen you.

Isaiah 49:6-7

King Herod

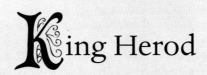

JERUSALEM

Now then, you kings, act wisely!
Be warned, you rulers of the earth!
Serve the LORD with reverent fear,
and rejoice with trembling.
Submit to God's royal son, or he will become angry,
and you will be destroyed in the midst of all your activities—
for his anger flares up in an instant.
But what joy for all who take refuge in him!

Psalm 2:10-12

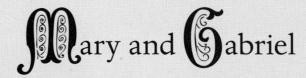Mary and Gabriel

OLIVE GROVE NEAR JERUSALEM

God sent the angel Gabriel to Nazareth, a village in Galilee, to a virgin named Mary. She was engaged to be married to a man named Joseph, a descendant of King David. Gabriel appeared to her and said, "Greetings, favored woman! The Lord is with you!" Confused and disturbed, Mary tried to think what the angel could mean. "Don't be afraid, Mary," the angel told her, "for you have found favor with God! You will conceive and give birth to a son, and you will name him Jesus. He will be very great and will be called the Son of the Most High. The Lord God will give him the throne of his ancestor David. And he will reign over Israel forever; his Kingdom will never end!"

Luke 1:26-33

Mary asked the angel,
"But how can this happen? I am a virgin."
The angel replied,
"The Holy Spirit will come upon you,
and the power of the Most High will overshadow you.
So the baby to be born will be holy,
and he will be called the Son of God. . . .
For nothing is impossible with God."

Luke 1:34-37

"I am the Lord's servant."

Luke 1:38

"Oh, how my soul praises the Lord.

How my spirit rejoices in God my Savior!

For he took notice of his lowly servant girl,

and from now on all generations will call me blessed.

For the Mighty One is holy,

and he has done great things for me.

He shows mercy from generation to generation

to all who fear him.

His mighty arm has done tremendous things!
He has scattered the proud and haughty ones.
He has brought down princes from their thrones
and exalted the humble.
He has filled the hungry with good things
and sent the rich away with empty hands.
He has helped his servant Israel
and remembered to be merciful.
For he made this promise to our ancestors,
to Abraham and his children forever."

Luke 1:46-55

"You have found favor with God!"

Luke 1:30

Mary and Elizabeth

HILL COUNTRY OF JUDEA

At the sound of Mary's greeting, Elizabeth's child leaped within her, and Elizabeth was filled with the Holy Spirit. Elizabeth gave a glad cry and exclaimed to Mary, "God has blessed you above all women, and your child is blessed. Why am I so honored, that the mother of my Lord should visit me? When I heard your greeting, the baby in my womb jumped for joy. You are blessed because you believed that the Lord would do what he said."

Luke 1:41-45

"God has blessed you above all women,
and your child is blessed."

Luke 1:42

Joseph

VILLAGE OF NAZARETH

Out of the stump of David's family will grow a shoot—
yes, a new Branch bearing fruit from the old root.
And the Spirit of the Lord will rest on him—
the Spirit of wisdom and understanding,
the Spirit of counsel and might,
the Spirit of knowledge and the fear of the LORD.

Isaiah 11:1-2

In that day the heir to David's throne
will be a banner of salvation to all the world.
The nations will rally to him,
and the land where he lives will be a glorious place.

Isaiah 11:10

God will establish one of David's descendants as king.
He will rule with mercy and truth.
He will always do what is just and be eager to do what is right.

Isaiah 16:5

Joseph . . . was a good man.

Matthew 1:19

John the Baptist

"You, my little son,
will be called the prophet of the Most High,
because you will prepare the way for the Lord.
You will tell his people how to find salvation
through forgiveness of their sins.
Because of God's tender mercy,
the morning light from heaven is about to break upon us,
to give light to those who sit in darkness and in the shadow of death,
and to guide us to the path of peace."

Luke 1:76-79

"I wonder what this child will turn out to be?
For the hand of the LORD is surely upon him in a special way."

Luke 1:66

"You are blessed because you believed that
the Lord would do what he said."

Luke 1:45

"Look! I am sending my messenger, and he will prepare the way before me. . . .
The messenger of the covenant, whom you look for so eagerly, is surely coming,"
says the LORD.

Malachi 3:1

Mary and Joseph

NAZARETH

Mary . . . was engaged to be married to Joseph. But before the marriage took place, while she was still a virgin, she became pregnant through the power of the Holy Spirit. Joseph, her fiancé, was a good man and did not want to disgrace her publicly, so he decided to break the engagement quietly.

Matthew 1:18-19

Joseph and Gabriel

NAZARETH

An angel of the Lord appeared to him in a dream. "Joseph, son of David," the angel said, "do not be afraid to take Mary as your wife. For the child within her was conceived by the Holy Spirit. And she will have a son, and you are to name him Jesus, for he will save his people from their sins."

Matthew 1:20-21

"He did as the angel of the Lord commanded."

Matthew 1:24

King Herod

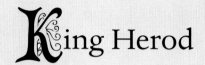

JUDEA

"A cry is heard in Ramah—
deep anguish and bitter weeping.
Rachel weeps for her children,
refusing to be comforted—
for her children are gone. . . .
Do not weep any longer,
for I will reward you," says the LORD.
"Your children will come back to you
from the distant land of the enemy.
There is hope for your future," says the LORD.
"Your children will come again to their own land."

Jeremiah 31:15-17

Herod's brutal action fulfilled what God had spoken.

Matthew 2:17

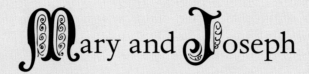

Mary and Joseph

THE ROAD TO BETHLEHEM

At that time the Roman emperor, Augustus, decreed that a census should be taken throughout the Roman Empire. (This was the first census taken when Quirinius was governor of Syria.) All returned to their own ancestral towns to register for this census. And because Joseph was a descendant of King David, he had to go to Bethlehem in Judea, David's ancient home. He traveled there from the village of Nazareth in Galilee. He took with him Mary, his fiancée, who was now obviously pregnant.

Luke 2:1-5

I will brighten the darkness before them and smooth out the road ahead of them. Yes, I will indeed do these things; I will not forsake them.

Isaiah 42:16

I am about to do something new. See, I have already begun!
Do you not see it? I will make a pathway through the wilderness.
I will create rivers in the dry wasteland.

Isaiah 43:19

You, O Bethlehem Ephrathah,
are only a small village among all the people of Judah.
Yet a ruler of Israel will come from you,
one whose origins are from the distant past.
The people of Israel will be abandoned to their enemies
until the woman in labor gives birth.
Then at last his fellow countrymen
will return from exile to their own land.

Micah 5:2-3

And while they were there,
the time came for her baby to be born.

Luke 2:6

Magi

TRAVELING TO BETHLEHEM

The people who walk in darkness
will see a great light.
For those who live in a land of deep darkness,
a light will shine.

Isaiah 9:2

Who among you fears the LORD and obeys his servant?
If you are walking in darkness, without a ray of light,
trust in the LORD and rely on your God.

Isaiah 50:10

"We have come to worship him."

Matthew 2:2

Zechariah and Elizabeth

JUDEA

Listen! It's the voice of someone shouting,
"Clear the way through the wilderness for the LORD!
Make a straight highway through the wasteland for our God!
Then the glory of the LORD will be revealed,
and all people will see it together.
The LORD has spoken!"

Isaiah 40:3, 5

"He will prepare the people for the coming of the Lord."

Luke 1:17

hepherds

A FIELD OUTSIDE BETHLEHEM

Suddenly, an angel of the Lord appeared among them, and the radiance of the Lord's glory surrounded them. They were terrified, but the angel reassured them. "Don't be afraid!" he said. "I bring you good news that will bring great joy to all people. The Savior—yes, the Messiah, the Lord—has been born today in Bethlehem, the city of David! And you will recognize him by this sign: You will find a baby wrapped snugly in strips of cloth, lying in a manger." Suddenly, the angel was joined by a vast host of others—the armies of heaven—praising God and saying,

"Glory to God in highest heaven,
and peace on earth to those with whom God is pleased."

Luke 2:9-14

"I bring you good news that will bring great joy to all people."

Luke 2:10

When the angels had returned to heaven, the shepherds said
to each other, "Let's go to Bethlehem! Let's see this thing that
has happened, which the Lord has told us about."

Luke 2:15

A Child Is Born

BETHLEHEM

For a child is born to us,
a son is given to us.
The government will rest on his shoulders.
And he will be called:
Wonderful Counselor, Mighty God,
Everlasting Father, Prince of Peace.
His government and its peace
will never end.
He will rule with fairness and justice from the throne
of his ancestor David for all eternity.

Isaiah 9:6-7

I will give you to my people, Israel,
as a symbol of my covenant with them.
And you will be a light to guide the nations.

Isaiah 42:6

God is with us!

Isaiah 8:10

Yet you brought me safely from my mother's womb
and led me to trust you at my mother's breast.
I was thrust into your arms at my birth.
You have been my God from the moment I was born.

Psalm 22:9-10

Mary kept all these things in her heart.

Luke 2:19

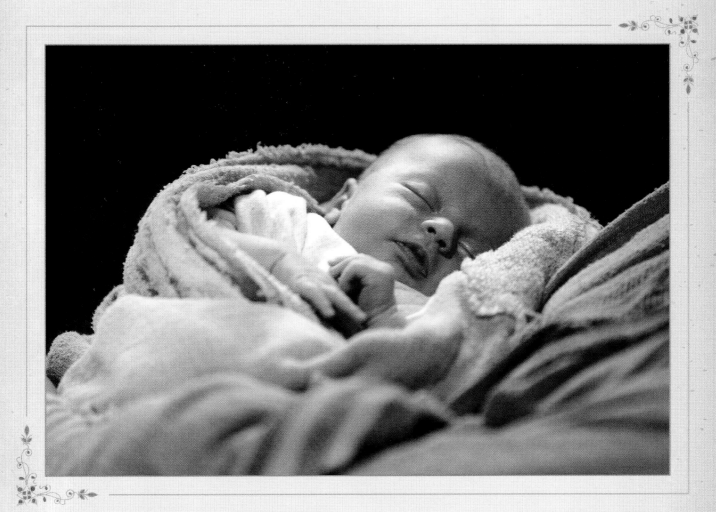

The Word became human and made his home among us.

John 1:14

Christ the Savior

BETHLEHEM

The star they had seen in the east guided them to Bethlehem. It went ahead of them and stopped over the place where the child was. When they saw the star, they were filled with joy! They entered the house and saw the child with his mother, Mary, and they bowed down and worshiped him. Then they opened their treasure chests and gave him gifts of gold, frankincense, and myrrh.

Matthew 2:9-11

The light shines in the darkness,
and the darkness can never extinguish it.

John 1:5

Silent Night

Silent night, holy night,
All is calm, all is bright
Round yon virgin mother and child.
Holy infant, so tender and mild,
Sleep in heavenly peace,
Sleep in heavenly peace.

Silent night, holy night,
Shepherds quake at the sight.
Glories stream from heaven afar,
Heavenly hosts sing alleluia!;
Christ the Savior is born!
Christ the Savior is born!

Silent night, holy night,
Son of God, love's pure light
Radiant beams from thy holy face,
With the dawn of redeeming grace
Jesus, Lord, at thy birth,
Jesus, Lord, at thy birth.

Silent night, holy night.
Wondrous star, lend thy light
With the angels let us sing,
Alleluia to our King.
Christ the Savior is born!
Christ the Savior is born!